BACK TO BASICS

READING

Catherine Hilton and Margaret Hyder

Acknowledgements

© 1993 National Extension College Trust Ltd

Reprinted 1995, 1996. Revised 1999. Reprinted 2002 with Assignments included.

ISBN 1 85356 444 3

Written by: Catherine Hilton and Margaret Hyder

Consultants: Michael Charles, Anne Dewsbury, Garth Freeman, Pauline Lawrence, and Margery Styles

Page design by: Squires Graphics

Cover design by: Information Design Workshop.

Printed by Pear Tree Press Limited, Stevenage

The publishers wish to acknowledge the following sources for material reproduced here: British Telecommunications plc: p15; Compaq Computers Ltd: p18; CTA Services, Swindon: p27; Dartmouth Publishing Company (*British Social Attitudes*): p42; Eyre Methuen Books Ltd: p33; Faber and Faber ('Money' from *High Windows*, by Philip Larkin): p42; *The Independent* and David Lister: p26; Longman Group UK (*Engineering Fundamentals*, R L Timings, 1988): p44; Nicholas Brealey Publishing, London (extract from *Are you Managing: a Guide to Good Management*, Peter Stemp (Allied Dunbar Management Series)): p25; Northern Foods plc: p25; Tesco Stores Ltd: p16; University of Derby: p23.

The extract from *The Birds* on p32 is reproduced with permission of Curtis Brown Ltd, London on behalf of The Chichester Partnership. Copyright 1952 by Daphne de Maurier.

No part of this publication may be reproduced, stored in a retrieval system, or transmitted in any form or by any means, electronic, mechanical, photocopying, recording, or otherwise, without the prior permission of the publisher.

The National Extension College is an educational trust and a registered charity with a distinguished body of trustees. It is an independent, self-financing organisation.

Since it was established in 1963, NEC has pioneered the development of flexible learning for adults. NEC is actively developing innovative materials and systems for distance learning opportunities on over 150 courses, from basic skills to degree and professional training.

For further details of NEC resources and supported courses, contact:

National Extension College Trust Ltd
The Michael Young Centre
Purbeck Road
Cambridge CB2 2HN
Tel. 01223 400200 Fax 01223 400399
Email: info@nec.ac.uk
Website: www.nec.ac.uk

Assignments

If you are studying *Back to Basics: Reading* with NEC as a course with tutor support then you must refer to the Assignments Booklet that accompanies it. If you are not studying *Back to Basics: Reading* with NEC and think that you might like to, you can obtain further details by contacting NEC, either in writing at the above address, or by telephoning 01223 400200.

Contents

	Mappings to key skills and basic skills specifications	i
	Introduction	5
Unit 1	**Introducing reading**	**7**
	What do you read?	7
	How do you approach reading?	8
	Why do you read?	9
	What do you need to improve?	9
Unit 2	**Skimming and scanning**	**10**
	What are skimming and scanning?	10
	Developing the skimming approach	14
	Developing the scanning approach	15
Unit 3	**Pitfalls**	**18**
	Tackling problem passages	18
	Understanding exam questions	22
Unit 4	**Points of view**	**24**
	Is it a fact?	25
	What is the writer's intention?	26
Unit 5	**Careful reading**	**29**
	Developing your understanding	30
	How can you improve your comprehension?	30
	Are you reading critically?	34
Unit 6	**Reading for research**	**35**
	Using your library	36
	Using reference books	37
	The layout of reference books	38
	Finding and recording information	39
Unit 7	**Study areas**	**41**
	English literature	41
	Sociology	42
	Geography	43
	Business studies	43
	Technology	43
Unit 8	**Reviewing progress**	**45**
	Reading and examinations	45
	What have you achieved?	47
	Making more opportunities	47
	Where next?	48
	Index	**49**

Mappings to key skills and basic skills specifications

The following grids show how *Back to Basics Reading* can be used to develop the skills needed for the Communication Key Skills at Levels 2 and 3 (1995 and 2000 specifications), and City & Guilds Wordpower Levels 2 and 3.

City & Guilds Wordpower Level 2

Unit 307: Read and respond to textual and graphical material

Underpinning knowledge and understanding	Unit
Purposes and expectations of different sorts of texts, charts and graphs	Unit 7 Study areas
Layout and indexing of source material	Unit 6 Reading for research
Appropriate context cueing can be used to obtain information	Unit 2 Skimming and scanning
Skimming, scanning and index skills are needed to find relevant information	Unit 2 Skimming and acanning
Interrelationships between text and graphical material	
Text can express fact and opinion	Unit 4 Points of view Unit 5 Careful reading
Language can be used emotively for a purpose	Unit 4 Points of view Unit 5 Careful reading
A case is made stronger by supporting evidence	
Purposes of reference systems	Unit 6 Reading for research
Information for reference needs to be structured in a logical way	
There are a number of different and equally logical ways of laying out information, including alphabetical order, numerical order, time order, sequence order etc.	
Abbreviations and prefixes	
'Signal' words aid searches for relevant material	Unit 2 Skimming and scanning

© National Extension College

City & Guilds Wordpower Level 3

Unit 310: Read and respond to textual and graphical material

Underpinning knowledge and understanding	Unit
Text is not always factual; it can be opinion	Unit 4 Points of view Unit 5 Careful reading
Language can be used emotively for a purpose	Unit 4 Points of view Unit 5 Careful reading
What to expect from different sorts of texts, graphs and charts	Unit 7 Study Areas
A case is made stronger by supportive evidence	
Not all sources are equally relevant	Unit 6 Reading for research
Layout and indexing of source materials provide clues to content	Unit 6 Reading for research
Appropriate context cues can be used to obtain information	Unit 2 Skimming and scanning
Skimming and scanning and index skills are used to locate relevant information	Unit 2 Skimming and scanning Unit 6 Reading for research
Relationships between texts	Unit 5 Careful reading
Purposes of using graphical material	
Specialist vocabulary of charts and graphs	
Relationship between text and graphical material	
How to interpret charts and graphs	
Purposes of reference systems	Unit 6 Reading for research
Different reference systems and how they are organised	Unit 6 Reading for research
Conventions of ordering related material	
Alphabetical/numerical, chronological, subject and geographical ordering	Unit 6 Reading for research
Abbreviations and prefixes	
Using 'signal' words aids material search	Unit 2 Skimming and scanning
Selection criteria to sort and classify data	
Appropriate referencing keys to be used	
How to sort related data into groups	

Key Skills Specifications (1995): Communication Level 2

Element 2.4: Read and respond to written materials

A student must:			Unit
Select and read materials for a purpose			Unit 1 Introducing reading Unit 6 Reading for research
Extract the necessary information for a purpose:			
	Identify and understand key points/ideas		Unit 3 Pitfalls Unit 4 Points of view Unit 5 Careful reading
	Extract the meaning accurately		Unit 3 Pitfalls Unit 4 Points of view Unit 5 Careful reading
Use appropriate sources of reference to clarify understanding of the subject:			
	Sources of reference	Using dictionaries	Unit 3 Pitfalls
		Reading instructions	
	Straightforward		
Summarise the information extracted:			
	In writing		Unit 4 Points of view Unit 5 Careful reading
	Orally		

Key Skills Specifications (1995): Communication Level 3

Element 3.4: Read and respond to written materials

A student must:			Unit
Select and read materials for a purpose			Unit 6 Reading for research Unit 1 Introducing reading
	Scanning		Unit 2 Skimming and scanning
	Skim-reading		Unit 2 Skimming and scanning
Extract the necessary information for a purpose			
	Identify and understand key points/ideas		Unit 3 Pitfalls
	Extract the meaning accurately		Unit 3 Pitfalls Unit 4 Points of view
Use appropriate sources of reference to clarify understanding of the subject			
	Sources of reference	Using dictionaries	Unit 3 Pitfalls
		Asking for clarification	
	Straightforward		
	Complex	Understanding of specialist vocabulary	Unit 5 Careful reading Unit 6 Reading for research
		Follow complex trains of thought	Unit 4 Points of view
		Form accurate judgements	Unit 4 Points of view
Summarise the information extracted:			
	In writing		Unit 4 Points of view Unit 5 Careful reading
	Orally		

Key Skills Specifications (2000): Communication Level 2

Part A: What you need to know

In reading and summarising information, YOU NEED TO KNOW HOW TO:	Unit
Use different sources to obtain relevant information	Unit 1 Introducing reading Unit 6 Reading for research
Skim materials to gain a general idea of content and scan text to identify the information you need from straightforward, extended documents	Unit 2 Skimming and scanning Unit 6 Reading for research
Recognise the writer's intentions	Unit 4 Points of view
Identify main lines of reasoning and main points from text and images	Unit 3 Pitfalls
Summarise information for a purpose	Unit 4 Points of view Unit 5 Careful reading

Key Skills Specifications (2000): Communication Level 3

Part A What you need to know

In reading and synthesising information, YOU NEED TO KNOW HOW TO:	Unit
Find and skim-read extended documents, such as text books, secondary sources, articles and reports, to identify relevant material	Unit 2 Skimming and scanning Unit 6 Reading for research
Scan and read the material to find the specific information you need	Unit 2 Skimming and scanning
Use appropriate sources of reference to help you understand complex lines of reasoning and information from text and images	Unit 1 Introducing reading Unit 3 Pitfalls Unit 6 Reading for research
Compare accounts and recognise opinion and possible bias	Unit 4 Points of view
Synthesise the information you have obtained for a purpose	Unit 4 Points of view Unit 5 Careful reading

INTRODUCTION

When we were preparing this material, it was our intention that you would work through all the units. We recommend that you use them in the order in which they occur. Each unit looks at specific reading skills and these skills fit together to make up the reading process.

You will need a good dictionary so that you can look up any word when you are unsure of its meaning. We suggest a concise dictionary such as:

Chambers Concise Dictionary

The Concise Oxford Dictionary

The New Penguin English Dictionary

Collins New Compact English Dictionary.

Before you begin work on the first unit, you will need:

- a notebook or some rough paper;
- a sheet of A4 paper or card at the ready to stop yourself reading the answers to activities before you have written down your own.

UNIT 1
INTRODUCING READING

Targets

This unit will help you to:

→ review what you read or need to read;

→ identify the variety of reading styles you use;

→ review your reasons for reading;

→ reflect upon the benefits of wide reading;

→ decide which aspects of your reading you need to improve.

Reading is an essential skill. Everyone has to read to cope with everyday life and work. Although we may spend time reading for pleasure, there are many occasions when we read because we have to. This means that there are plenty of opportunities to practise reading, but this practice does not automatically improve our skills. In this course we are going to look at how you can practise reading in a way that helps you to:

■ become a more efficient and effective reader;

■ gain more enjoyment from the things that you read.

What do you read?

A good starting point is to think about the different things that you read. Here are some notes about some of the reading one of us did yesterday:

1 Early morning:

 (a) skipped through letter from my aunt to see what time she would be arriving on Sunday;

 (b) read letter from DSS about voluntary pension contributions. Didn't fully understand it – will read it again later;

 (c) used telephone directory to find number for Leeds Station.

2 At work:

 (a) read new exam regulations and highlighted main points for future reference;

 (b) read a report and noted down main points to discuss at meeting;

 (c) quickly read a memo about car parking so that I could see what it was about.

3   At home:

   (a) glanced at two leaflets on doormat and disregarded them (I don't need double glazing, nor do I want my carpets steam cleaned!);

   (b) looked briefly at local newspaper headlines and read articles which I thought would interest me;

   (c) continued reading *Paradise News* by David Lodge – couldn't put it down.

Activity

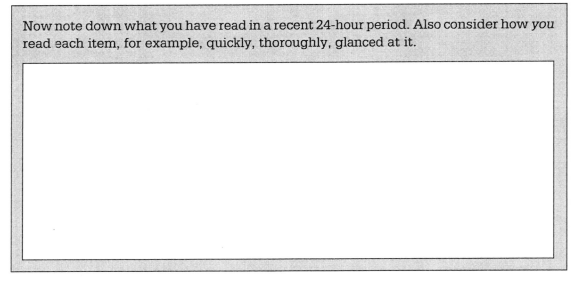

Now note down what you have read in a recent 24-hour period. Also consider how *you* read each item, for example, quickly, thoroughly, glanced at it.

You probably included a whole range of reading materials: letters, postcards, exam papers, reports, adverts, newspapers, magazines, recipes, instructions, manuals, notices, labels, signs, essays, assignments, books, reference materials.

You may also have included maps, plans, charts, graphs and diagrams, or perhaps you don't think of these as reading tasks.

How do you approach reading?

Let's reflect further on our list of reading activities and yours. The different reading materials involved different approaches to reading. The chances are that you did some or all of the following:

- glanced at something quickly to see what it was about (see the discussion on 'skimming' in Unit 2);

- studied something closely in order to understand it in detail;

- looked through something to find a particular piece of information (see the discussion on 'scanning' in Unit 2);

- read a difficult passage slowly or more than once in order to understand it;

- read something carefully to find the main points;

- read something for pleasure and enjoyment.

We'll be returning to these different approaches in later units.

Why do you read?

Activity

We have already suggested some of the reasons for reading. Perhaps you would like to make a list of these reasons and add any others you can think of. Use your notebook for this.

You may have noted down:
- to find the main points in a document;
- to find a particular piece of information;
- to follow instructions;
- to get the gist of something;
- for study purposes;
- to understand, so that you can tell someone else about what you have read, or as a basis for discussion;
- to enjoy a story;
- to find out other people's views.

As you have seen, we read a wide range of materials for many different reasons and we adopt a number of approaches to reading. Our approach depends on both our reason for reading and what we are reading. For example, if we need to gain information from a piece of writing which is difficult to understand, we read slowly and will probably read it, or parts of it, more than once.

Before you start to read a particular passage, think carefully about your reason for reading and what you want to gain from reading it. In this way you will be able to improve your reading skills and become a more competent reader.

What do you need to improve?

Activity

Here are some examiners' complaints about candidates' reading. Read them through and place a tick next to any that apply to you:

Candidates fail to:
- pay attention to the word 'explain' ☐
- read thoroughly ☐
- draw generalisations from what they read ☐
- read questions exactly ☐
- recognise what is asked ☐
- gather sufficient relevant ideas from a passage. ☐

Activity

The following lists include the main requirements for effective reading. You may care to put a tick beside those which apply to you:

Reading may require us to:
- concentrate ☐
- understand what we read ☐
- understand passages written in different styles. ☐

Sometimes we have to:
- read quickly ☐
- make notes about what we've read ☐
- summarise what we've read ☐
- find a specific reference ☐
- remember what we've read ☐
- make judgements ☐
- keep a reading diary ☐
- compare one piece of writing with another ☐
- extract information from a number of different sources ☐
- use reference books ☐
- consider the writer's purpose (for example, is he/she trying to persuade or influence?). ☐

Now review this list again. Do you need to plan further work in order to meet any of these requirements? You may find it helpful to consider which are most important to you, then list them in priority order so that you can deal with your most important ones first. You could prepare an action plan as follows:

ACTION PLAN
1
2
3
4
5
6
7

Review

Reading widens your horizons. We would advise you to read as much as possible and to read a wide variety of materials. For example, you could plan:

- background reading for study purposes;
- background reading for work purposes;
- reading for general knowledge;
- reading for relaxation and pleasure.

If you are serious about improving your reading skills, you will need to set aside time specifically for reading as it can all too easily be crowded out. Approach reading in an organised way:

- Set time aside each day.
- Find a room where you won't be disturbed and can concentrate.
- Have a notebook so that you can jot down things of interest or importance.
- Use a dictionary so that you can look up words that you are uncertain about.
- Keep a reading diary where you can record details of titles, authors and perhaps your comments about each book you read. This will be particularly useful if you are studying.

Reading, as well as giving pleasure and information, has other advantages:

- It allows you to see how other people write.
- You will notice how they punctuate their work.
- You will observe how words are spelt.
- You will become aware of different styles of writing.
- You will see a wide variety of vocabulary being used.

UNIT 2
SKIMMING AND SCANNING

Targets

This unit will help you to:

→ understand the importance of skimming and scanning;

→ develop these approaches to reading;

→ practise using skimming and scanning.

In Unit 1 you saw that the term 'reading' covers a number of different activities. In this unit you look at two of these, skimming and scanning. You will consider why you might use these approaches and how you can use them effectively.

What are skimming and scanning?

Activity

You will probably be aware of other situations when we use the words 'skim' and 'scan', for example:

- *skimmed* milk;
- having a health *scan*.

Use a sheet in your notebook to jot down your ideas about the meanings of 'skim' and 'scan' and then check the two words in your dictionary.

Your dictionary may suggest that the words have very similar meanings. Students sometimes find it difficult to see the difference between skimming and scanning. However, when applied to reading, to *skim* is to read superficially. If you skim through a book you will get the gist of it and will be able to describe the subject matter in general terms, but you will not be able to give many details. On the other hand, to *scan* is to search through a text for a specific item of information. You will ignore anything that is irrelevant and concentrate on finding exactly what you are looking for.

Sometimes you may combine these two approaches to reading: skimming first to get the gist and then scanning for a specific point. It doesn't matter if, when you have completed this unit, you forget the precise meanings of these two words, provided you remember the difference between the two approaches and use the appropriate approach for the task.

Activity

Look at the following list of reading tasks. Tick beneath each whether you would use skimming, scanning or a combination of the two approaches:

1. finding a friend's number in a telephone directory

   ☐ skim   ☐ scan   ☐ a combination

2. choosing a novel to read for pleasure

   ☐ skim   ☐ scan   ☐ a combination

3. deciding whether a sociology textbook would help you to write an essay about parenting in Britain today

   ☐ skim   ☐ scan   ☐ a combination

4. looking up the temperature for roast beef in a table showing correct oven temperatures

   ☐ skim   ☐ scan   ☐ a combination

5. using a workshop manual to find the correct tyre pressure for your car

   ☐ skim   ☐ scan   ☐ a combination

6. deciding whether to buy a local newspaper

   ☐ skim   ☐ scan   ☐ a combination

7. looking at a holiday brochure to see which countries it covers

   ☐ skim   ☐ scan   ☐ a combination

8. looking at an exam timetable to find out the time of your English exam

   ☐ skim   ☐ scan   ☐ a combination

9. looking at a menu outside a restaurant to decide whether you want to eat there.

   ☐ skim   ☐ scan   ☐ a combination

Our suggestions are:

- telephone directory: you'll know the name of your friend so you'll scan the guide words at the top of each page to find the correct page, and then scan the columns to find your friend's name;

- choosing a novel: you'll skim through to see whether you've read it before, to get the gist of the story and to see whether the writer's style appeals to you;

- sociology textbook: you may skim through to check whether it might be appropriate and then scan the index to see whether it covers parenting;

- oven setting: scan through to find 'roast beef' then read off the temperature;
- tyre pressures: probably scan through the index for 'tyre pressures', refer to the correct page then scan the page to find the correct pressure;
- newspaper: probably skim through looking at headlines, pictures, news stories to gain a general impression;
- holiday brochure: skim through to gain general impression of countries included and then look in more detail;
- exam timetable: scan to find the subject and then read off the time (you may have to skim first to see how the timetable is organised, that is, in subject or date order);
- menu: skim to see the types of meals offered (and the cost!).

You may have different ideas from ours (for instance, you may be a 'foodie' and want to study the menu in detail before you go in) but if you are skilled in using these two approaches to reading you should be able to find information more quickly and effectively.

Developing the skimming approach

As you saw in the previous activity, you will often skim when you want to make a decision about a book, magazine, article, etc. If you are to skim in a meaningful way, you need to think about the parts of the material which will be most useful to you. These differ according to the material you are considering.

Activity

Turn to Unit 3. You are going to decide whether it is likely to be of interest or use to you. What parts of Unit 3 would be particularly helpful to look at as you skim through it?

We would look at the title, the targets, the headings and then briefly skim through the introductory paragraph of each section.

Activity

You are trying to decide whether to buy a new magazine that deals with a subject that interests you. What sort of things would you look at as you skimmed through it?

As we skimmed through it, we would look at: layout, names of writers, use of photographs, number of pages, number of adverts, titles of articles, headings. We would also skim through one or two articles to get the gist and the flavour of them.

Although when you skim you won't linger on anything too long, you will want to gain something from the activity and be able to retain an overview of the material.

Activity

Skim through the following advert for 'Talking Pages'. Follow the points about skimming that we have outlined and then below the extract jot down what you've learnt about the service.

When there's a business or service you need, there's a quick and easy way to find it. Call **TALKING PAGES** and let our friendly staff guide you to what you require.

For all types of businesses...

Talking Pages is an established telephone service which will give you up-to-date information on services, shops and businesses – anywhere in the country – 24 hours a day, 365 days a year – and it only costs a normal rate call.

...and all types of information

We'll give you information on everything from electricians to employment agencies, sports shops to surveyors – in fact, all the same sorts of categories that you can find in **YELLOW PAGES** ®. As well as the name, address and telephone number, in many cases we can also give you details of opening times, payment methods, parking facilities, products and services – and much more.

For all types of people

Talking pages is for everyone! Whether you're calling from home, from work, from a mobile phone or from a public call box, we're here and ready to help you, offering information across the U.K. Cellnet users can call Talking Pages on 888.

Easy to use service

We've enclosed a diary card for your wallet and some stickers for your telephone, address book or diary. So, keep our number handy and the next time you need a printer in Plumstead... a hotel at Heathrow... or a takeaway in Tottenham – simply pick up the phone and dial our number!

When we skimmed through we gained this ipression:

'Talking Pages' is a telephone service which gives the caller information on businesses throughout the country. This information is similar to that shown in Yellow Pages. Anyone can use the service.

Developing the scanning approach

You've already seen that scanning involves you in concentrating on finding a specific item. In order to home in on one item you will need to feel confident that you can find the relevant page or passage efficiently.

READING

Activity

Think about looking up the name and phone number of a local plumber in a Yellow Pages directory. What do you need to know about Yellow Pages in order to do this?

Note down your ideas before continuing.

Our suggestions are that you may need to know about: the layout of the directory, including the index at the back; alphabetical order; the types of headings used.

Activity

You want to find out the saturated fat content of the following products, listed in the table below: frozen shepherd's pie; vanilla ice-cream; natural yoghurt. What do you need to know about the table below in order to be able to scan it for these products? Look at the table and then note down what you need to know.

TESCO OWN LABEL PRODUCTS		TYPICAL FAT CONTENT AS GRAMS PER 100g		
		TOTAL FAT	SATURATED FAT	POLYUNSATURATED FAT
CAKES	Dairy Cream Doughnuts	19.1	9.2	1.8
	Raspberry Jam Sponge Sandwich	7.3	1.6	1.0
	Fruited Teacakes	4.6	1.9	1.0
CHEESE	Cheddar	34.4	22.7	1.1
	Healthy Eating Half Fat Cheese (Cheddar Type)	15.0	9.9	0.5
	Full Fat Soft Cheese	29.7	19.8	0.8
	Healthy Eating Low Fat Soft Cheese	6.8	4.9	0.1
	Natural Cottage Cheese	3.9	2.4	0.1
DESSERT TOPPINGS	Fresh Double Cream	48.0	31.7	1.5
	Fresh Single Cream	19.1	12.6	0.6
	Fresh Half Cream	13.3	8.8	0.4
	Natural Yogurt	0.8	0.5	Trace
	Healthy Eating Natural Fromage Frais	Trace	Trace	Trace
DESSERTS	Frozen Blackcurrant Cheesecake	13.7	9.0	0.6
	Frozen Bramley Apple Pie	8.5	4.7	0.7
	Vanilla Ice Cream Brick	6.5	3.5	0.2
	Low Fat Strawberry Yogurt	1.0	0.6	Trace
FISH	Frozen Cod Fillet in Ovencrisp Breadcrumbs	7.1	1.4	4.1
	Frozen Health Eating Cod Fillet in Ovencrisp Breadcrumbs	2.5	0.4	1.5
	Cod Fillet	0.6	0.2	0.3
MILK	Pasteurised Milk	3.9	2.6	0.1
	Healthy Eating Half Fat Milk	1.6	1.1	Trace
	Healthy Eating Virtually Fat Free Milk	0.1	0.1	Trace
OILS AND COOKING FATS	Lard	100.0	41.6	14.2
	Olive Oil	100.0	13.0	15.0
	Sunflower Oil	100.0	12.0	65.0
SALAD DRESSINGS	Mayonnaise	80.7	12.6	50.9
	Salad Cream	33.8	4.3	16.7
	Reduced Calorie Mayonnaise	33.8	4.7	16.7
	Reduced Calorie Salad Dressing	9.9	1.1	6.1
SAVOURIES	Chilled Premium Pork Sausage (grilled)	21.0	7.8	1.9
	Chilled Premium Low Fat Pork Sausage (grilled)	8.4	2.7	1.4
	Chilled Cornish Pasty	14.1	3.7	1.8
	Frozen Shepherds Pie	4.8	2.1	0.2
	Chilled Healthy Eating Vegetable Pizza	4.9	3.1	0.4
SPREADING FATS	Butter	81.7	54.0	2.6
	Sunflower Margarine	81.6	12.9	43.2
	Healthy Eating Half Fat Spread	40.0	7.3	18.0
	Healthy Eating Very Low Fat Spread	20.0	3.6	4.0

We think that you would need to know that: amounts for saturated fats are shown in the second column (look for heading 'saturated fats'); products are shown under general headings which are arranged in alphabetical order; products are not given in any particular order.

Activity

> Now list the steps you would take to scan the table for the information. Remember you want 'to home in' on those three products only.

For each product in turn, we would:

- think about the most likely heading for it;
- scan down the list under that heading;
- find the product;
- look across to the second column and find the amount.

You may have expected to find natural yoghurt under desserts, but when you couldn't find it under that you would need to think of an alternative heading.

If you think that you might take too long when scanning or find it difficult to concentrate on one aspect of the text, then you need to practise. As you have seen, it also helps to think about the task and how to tackle it before you start.

Activity

> Note down how you would use your dictionary efficiently to find the meanings of these words (don't bother to write down the meanings):
>
>   plough   embellish   poignant   skimp.
>
> You might also like to time yourself as you look for them.

You will find words more quickly in your dictionary if you are confident about alphabetical order and use the guide words at the top of each page to help you select the correct page. You also need to keep a strong visual image of the word in mind as you scan down the column.

Review

Having worked through this unit, you will be aware that it is important to use the right approach for the task you are doing. You will waste time and effort if you read through something carefully when you really need to skim or scan it. On the other hand, if you use a skimming or scanning approach for most of your reading, you might fail to be sufficiently thorough when you need to be. Before you start any reading task it is helpful to:

- think about why you are doing it;
- think about what you want to achieve;
- use skimming or scanning if they are appropriate.

UNIT 3

PITFALLS

Targets

This unit will help you to:

→ consider why some materials are difficult to read and understand;

→ find ways of overcoming these difficulties;

→ develop your confidence in tackling the more difficult passages.

In Unit 1 we referred to reading tasks in which you need to read a passage slowly and perhaps more than once in order to understand it fully. In this unit you are going to consider why certain passages may pose problems.

Tackling problem passages

Activity

Look at each of the following extracts. You may feel that all, or most, of them are difficult to understand. In the space below each extract, note down *why* the passage is difficult.

Extract 1:

Now the Contura 3/25c has won *PC Magazine's* prestigious Technical Innovation Award for the best Portable System regardless of price. So, more than ever, you can be confident your money's being well spent – especially when the Contura's low price includes a 25MHz 386SL processor, 84Mb or 120Mb Fixed Disk Drive, 4Mb of RAM, a Compaq trackball, Microsoft Windows 3.1, MS DOS 5.0, the latest management features and a three-year warranty.

Extract 2:

The Honorary Treasurer shall cause proper accounts to be kept and these shall be audited by the auditors who shall certify the correctness of the same and the said accounts so certified shall be published to the members of the Association once a year in time for consideration at Conference together with any remarks, notes or comments which the auditors may require there to be inserted therein. The Honorary Treasurer shall, whenever so required, deliver to the Executive a statement of all monies disbursed.

(From *NASUWT* Diary, 1992)

(continued opposite)

Extract 3:

With the comprehensive Midlands network of Motorways and 'A' Roads, together with a Rail Station directly linked to the airport Terminal Building via the 'MAGLEV' shuttle link plus a comprehensive local bus and rail network, BIRMINGHAM INTERNATIONAL AIRPORT lies at the centre of the best communications links within the United Kingdom.

(From Birmingham International Airport *Travel Information*)

Extract 4:

The messenger rode back at an easy trot, stopping pretty often at ale-houses by the way to drink, but evincing a tendency to keep his own counsel, and to keep his hat cocked over his eyes. He had eyes that assorted well with the decoration, being of a surface black, with no depth in the colour or form, and much too near together – as if they were afraid of being found out in something, singly, if they kept too far apart.

(From *A Tale of Two Cities*, by Charles Dickens)

You may have noted down similar reasons to these:

Extract 1: Difficult if you haven't a background knowledge about computers; technical information and vocabulary; unfamiliar abbreviations.

Extract 2: Formal, impersonal style; the language of official documents; don't fully understand the meaning of some of the words; long sentences; lack of punctuation.

Extract 3: Very long sentence; poorly punctuated.

Extract 4: Written in an unfamiliar style; not sure about the meaning of certain words and expressions.

Activity

If you were in a situation where it was necessary to understand each of the extracts above, what would you do to make each one easier to understand? Spend five to ten minutes thinking about this and make notes before comparing your notes with our suggestions.

You could:

1 Read the passage thoroughly.
2 Do some background reading.
3 Split the passage into parts.
4 Put the passage in to your own words.
5 Find out what the words mean.

Although we have numbered these points 1–5, there is no need to carry them out in that order. The number of steps and the order in which you follow them will depend on the passage you are reading. Bear this in mind as you read through the following notes.

Read the passage thoroughly

When you are presented with difficult piece of writing, you may find it helps to follow a procedure.

Activity

Here are some actions you could take. Number the actions 1–5, in order of priority.

(a) Highlight the words, sentences or parts of sentences which are difficult. ☐

(b) Read again the whole passage or the sections that are particularly difficult. ☐

(c) Next decide which further steps you need to take. ☐

(d) Read slowly and carefully. ☐

(e) Go back and read the easier parts again. Can you gain any meaning from these? ☐

We would put the actions in this order: d, b, a, e, c.

Do some background reading

Wide reading over a variety of good-quality materials will give you a background knowledge over a range of subjects, but it isn't only reading that will help you.

Activity

What else can you do to gain a good general knowledge about a variety of subjects? Note down your ideas before continuing.

You may have suggested:

- TV and radio – watching and listening to news, current affairs, documentaries and discussion programmes;
- listening to and talking with others so that you can exchange information and opinions.

If you have to read about an unfamiliar subject or study a new subject, acquire some background information first. Go to your local or college library and see what is available. You may feel very enthusiastic about your research and anxious to know as much as possible, but don't choose books which are too detailed or complicated. You can progress to these later. Initially you need clear background information about the subject. You could begin by looking at encyclopaedias to gain an overall picture or a dictionary of specialised terms so that you understand the vocabulary used. There will be more about researching for information in Unit 6.

Split the passage into parts

Look back at Extract 3 on page 19. The sentence is so long that it is difficult to spot what it is all about. A passage with too many long sentences can be very daunting to read. However, a long sentence will generally be divided into parts by commas. The commas mark off asides and additional pieces of information. Such 'asides' may occur at the beginning, middle or end of a sentence.

Activity

Use the commas in Extract 3 as a guide to:
- identify the extra pieces of information – underline each of these;
- identify the main message – note down what this is.

You probably wrote down 'BIRMINGHAM INTERNATIONAL AIRPORT lies at the centre of the best communications links within the United Kingdom'. The rest of the sentence supports this, giving details of the roads and railways.

When you need to tackle a long sentence, always remove the extra pieces of information first so that you can concentrate on understanding the main message. You can then go back and work on each 'aside'.

Put the passage into your own words

Even when you have taken a sentence apart, you may still find it difficult to understand. If you were passing on the main message of Extract 3 to someone, you might say something like this:

> Birmingham International Airport has excellent road and rail links.

We have expressed the message in our own words. We have 'translated' the writer's words into something which is more acceptable and meaningful to us. You will have the chance to try this out as you work through the next section.

Find out what the words mean

You may not have fully understood the meaning of some of the words in the extracts. It's a good idea to try to guess what they mean by looking at how they are used in the passage. You can then use a dictionary to check your guess.

Activity

Use a dictionary to look up the meanings of the following words from Extract 2:

audited:

auditor:

certify/certified:

inserted:

disbursed:

If you find the definitions in your dictionary difficult to follow, try to put them into your own words.

You may have written similar definitions to these:

- audited – checked;
- auditor – a person who checks accounts;
- certify or certified the correctness – say or declare they are correct;
- inserted – put in;
- disbursed – paid out.

It often helps to consult more than one dictionary so that if a definition in one dictionary is difficult to follow, you can then look it up in another.

Activity

Look through Extracts 1, 3 and 4 on pages 18–19. List the words you are uncertain about and then look them up in your dictionary. Don't forget to see if you can make a rough guess about their meanings first.

Activity

Now that you understand the meaning of all the words in Extract 4, you could try putting the main message into your own words. This may help you to understand it better. Do this now before comparing notes with our suggestion.

We wrote:

> As the messenger rode back, he stopped quite frequently for a drink at pubs on the way. He didn't mix with the people there and kept his hat over his eyes. His eyes were dark and far too close together.

You won't have used the same words, but we hope you gained the same understanding.

Extract 1 on page 18 is difficult because it uses abbreviations and technical terms. Your dictionary may not list all of these. If computing is not a subject in which you specialise then this may not matter. However, your work or studies may involve other groups of specialist terms. If so, it may be worthwhile acquiring a specialist dictionary to help you with these, if you have not done so already.

Activity

There are many specialist dictionaries. You may find it useful to check, in your college or public libraries and in good bookshops, to see what is available in your subject area.

Understanding exam questions

Some people have problems reading exam questions because they feel nervous and are aware that they must read quickly so as not to waste time. If you are like this, bear in mind that, though you may feel under pressure, it is vital to read slowly, thoroughly and carefully. This applies particularly to the exam questions themselves. If you read too quickly, you may miss vital words or misunderstand the question. Take this example:

UNIT 3 PITFALLS

> Drawing on the observations you have carried out in schools, your work in Educational Studies and your reading, indicate what you consider to be the advantages and disadvantages of class teaching, group work and individualised work in relation to two children, chosen from those you know well in the curriculum areas of English, Maths or Science.

Activity

Make a list of all the things the above question asks you to do.

We hope you included the following points:
- refer to: observations, work in Educational Studies, reading;
- choose two children;
- select English, Maths or Science;
- discuss advantages and disadvantages of:
  - class teaching;
  - group work;
  - individualised work.

> BY THE WAY
> - It is particularly important to pay attention to words such as 'and' and 'or'. Otherwise you could have made a careless mistake in the question above and written about all three: English, Maths and Science!
> - Pay attention to numbers, too, for example, *two* children; refer to *three* areas.

Review

- You might now like to go back to the activity on page 18 and see if you want to add to, or change, your suggestions about the way you would tackle each of the four passages.
- To round off your work on this unit we suggest you find a difficult passage in a newspaper, magazine or book and use it to apply the points that you have learnt.

UNIT 4

POINTS OF VIEW

Targets

This unit will help you to:

→ think about the writer's intentions in writing the material you are reading;

→ make judgements about what you read.

In this unit we want you to take a critical look at what you read and ask yourself:

- Is it fact?
- Is it opinion?
- Is it deliberately trying to be persuasive?
- Does it contain any emotive language?

Activity

To begin with we would like you to think about the meaning of the terms that we will be using in this unit. Note down brief definitions of the following words. Use your dictionary to help you:

Fact:

Opinion:

Persuade:

Emotive:

Here are our suggestions:

- A *fact* is something that is true: a truth.
- An *opinion* is a person's judgement or views.
- To *persuade* is to convince by argument.
- Anything described as *emotive* will tend to arouse emotions.

So:

- A factual piece of writing contains statements of truth.
- A passage with opinions in it contains a person's views.
- A persuasive piece of writing uses arguments to convince us to adopt a particular opinion or attitude.
- Emotive language in a piece of writing has been chosen to arouse our emotions so that we will share the writer's feelings.

When you think about these types of writing, you will see that a skilful writer can have a powerful influence upon us. It is therefore important for us, as readers, to look critically at any piece of writing to determine the writer's intentions.

Is it a fact?

How often have you heard someone say, 'I know it's true – I read it in the paper/I read it in a book'? We are apt to believe that what we see in print is true or factual whereas much of it is other people's views, hearsay or even gossip!

Activity

Look at the two extracts below and jot down which parts of each you think are factual and which you think are opinion. You could underline the parts in different colours to show the difference.

Extract 1:

You don't have to be superhuman to be a Manager. It often strengthens others' respect for you if you admit that you don't know something. You're not expected to know it all! It is also better to ask for help than to fail for want of it. We all need assistance at some time, so there's no need to feel inadequate. It's often useful and beneficial to share your problems with other Managers or your boss. No-one has the monopoly of all the good ideas and right answers, and inputs from others can often lead to superior solutions.

Extract 2:

Park Cakes baked a cake for a double celebration.

It was to recognise the thousandth person on the Oldham site to complete the Northern Foods basic food safety course and the thousandth to undertake Park Cakes' own safety training course.

A celebration cake was made and decorated by Brenda Skelton, of the test bakery, in the form of a machine isolation unit, representing one of the points of safe systems – 'Switch off and isolate before you clean.'

You probably decided that Extract 1 was entirely the writer's opinion. Most of his advice probably has some truth in it. For example, most of us may agree that 'It is ... better to ask for help than to fail.' But the writer is expressing what he *believes* to be true rather than something that can be proved as a fact.

Extract 2 is factual. You could prove that all of these things did take place. For example: Park Cakes baked a cake; the cake was made and decorated by Brenda Skelton.

Although some of the passages we read will be entirely factual and others will consist wholly of opinions, we will also read passages where fact and opinion appear side-by-side.

READING

Activity

Read the following passage and then make a list of all the **facts** that it contains:

> Brenda Lee is 4ft 9in tall; she turned down an invitation to sing for President Clinton because she was too busy – she is playing Brentwood Leisure Centre in Essex tonight; she possesses several hundred pairs of shoes, all size 5 ; 18 dolls' houses occupy the top storey of her home in Nashville; and she talks of her late friend Elvis Presley as a 'nice, shy, good family man'.
>
> One thing child stars now approaching middle-age have in common is a different perspective on life from the rest of us.

The whole of the first paragraph is fact except for 'nice, shy, good family man'. This is her opinion of Elvis Presley. Perhaps we could debate whether being 'too busy' was true or not! In the second paragraph the journalist presents his opinion on child stars approaching middle-age.

What is the writer's intention?

Activity

Look back at Extracts 1 and 2 in the activity before last. What is the writer's intention in each? Make a note of your ideas before continuing.

Our view is that the intention of the first writer is to give his readers confidence and convince them that they can cope as managers whereas the intention of the second writer is to give information about what has been happening at Park Cakes.

Activity

Now look at the following advert. What would you say is the writer's intention here?

> PEACEFUL AUTUMN HOLIDAYS
> Quiet roads and beautiful scenery in the Peak District National Park.
> Ideal for walkers. Hearty home cooking. All bedrooms en-suite in family-run hotel. Single rooms available. Any 2 days DBB £63 p.p.
> 5 days £150 p.p.
> Write to: Peak Bank Hotel, Thorpe, Derbyshire.

The writer is trying to persuade us to stay at the Peak Bank Hotel. We are given facts about the hotel (en-suite bedrooms, etc.) but also opinions (quiet roads, beautiful scenery) to help persuade us.

26

Advertisements aim to persuade us to buy products or use services. Although advertisers by law cannot lie about these, they can use language skilfully so that they appeal to our emotions and persuade us that we need their product or service.

Sometimes it isn't easy to spot a writer's intention, particularly if he or she uses convincing arguments.

Activity

Study the letter below and then note down your responses to the following questions:

- What is the writer's intention?
- When does the writer's intention become clear?
- How does the writer support his viewpoint?

> In reply to the letter from Mr T. Holden-Brown (*Construction Weekly*, 24 Feb.), it has to be said that commercial training organisations charge around £200/day for public courses because that is what they cost. Pricing down may mean that a few more people attend but, in the end, you simply make bigger losses at a faster rate.
>
> The problem stems from the days when training was heavily subsidised. Even colleges and universities are now required to be commercial. Contractors, which pay a levy to the CBI, get the benefit of grant aid but consultants, which do not support an industry training organisation, cannot expect to get something for nothing.
>
> We must consider tutors and lecturers. These are usually people who run successful businesses, and are not going to give away their hard-earned knowledge for nothing just to train competitors.
>
> If you think training is expensive, try ignorance. Read the other letters in last week's *Construction Weekly* and other comments about subbie bashing. How often do subcontractors fail because they do not know and do not follow the proper contractual procedures? They must still show exactly when they did extra work and provide evidence to prove contractual entitlement. There is a simple rule: what you can't prove you don't get.
>
> On this subject, we will soon be providing economical training for subcontractors through CITB – and it will not cost £200/day. Equally, much of the training we organise costs clients about £50–£60/day. It is not only large consultants and contractors that can benefit from in-house training.
>
> We have repeatedly offered to sell to smaller consultants low-cost training if they will get together into groups and form co-operatives.

At first it appears that the writer is supporting training costing £200. He gives a variety of reasons why organisations charge this amount. In paragraph 3 he tries to convince us of the value of training. By paragraph 4 his intention appears to have changed and he is advertising his own organisation, which provides cheaper training.

Activity

Writers, particularly in the popular press, often use emotive language to encourage readers to share their viewpoints. Read the following article and see if you can underline the words which seem to have deliberately been chosen to make the reader feel sympathy for the victim:

> On May 5th heartless thieves broke into a frail widower's flat in Rushley and stole his hard-earned savings. The man, who was too terrified to be named, recognised one of his ruthless attackers. 'He's one of a gang of louts who hangs around the local shops intimidating pensioners.'

You may have chosen: 'heartless', 'frail widower's', 'hard-earned', 'too terrified to be named', 'ruthless', 'gang', 'louts', 'hang around', 'intimidating'. All of these words and phrases are emotive.

Review

Careful reading involves more than just reading words and understanding them. It involves questioning what we read, thinking about the writer's standpoint and making judgements. You can now build on these skills by working through Unit 5, 'Careful Reading'.

UNIT 5
CAREFUL READING

Targets

This unit will help you to:
→ review your comprehension skills;
→ improve your comprehension skills;
→ read more critically.

In this unit we are going to continue to look at the importance of effective reading. We will do this by considering the many occasions when it is essential to gain real and deep meaning from texts, for example, documents at work, books for study purposes, official correspondence, exam questions and texts.

Activity

We have already considered some of the activities that make up careful reading. Spend five to ten minutes thinking about the suggestions that you have encountered so far in this study guide and making a list of these in your notebook. You'll need to focus particularly on Units 3 and 4.

You may have noted some or all of the following:

- choosing the right reading approach;
- thinking about your purpose for reading;
- concentration;
- dealing with difficult or unfamiliar vocabulary;
- understanding different styles of writing;
- breaking up long sentences;
- working out the writer's intention;
- distinguishing fact from opinion;
- recognising persuasion and emotive language;
- first skimming through to get an overall impression of a piece of writing.

We are now going to add to this list by considering further what is involved in understanding a passage.

Developing your understanding

There is, of course, no point in reading unless we understand what we read. From an early age you will have been used to people asking you questions about what you have read.

Activity

If you really understand a passage, what should you be able to do after you have read it? Think about this for a few moments and list your ideas before continuing.

Don't worry if you haven't included all of the following:

- remember what you have read, both immediately and some time later;
- understand the significance of what you've read;
- be able to decide which are the main points and which are the minor or supplementary points;
- make deductions and judgements;
- draw conclusions;
- comment critically on what you've read;
- relate your reading to other knowledge you have on the subject;
- discuss what you've read or answer questions about it
- summarise the passage or make notes.

Activity

If you feel that any of these are difficult for you at the moment, list them so that you can come back to them later. You should then be able to decide how you can use the advice given in the unit to improve these aspects of your comprehension.

How can you improve your comprehension?

When presented with a passage, you should try to answer the following questions:

- Why are you reading it?
- What type of passage is it?
- What is the structure of the passage?

Let's consider each of these more fully.

Why are you reading a passage?

You should always question your purpose for reading anything.

- Do you expect it to give you:
  - an overall view?
  - detailed information?
  - facts/opinions?
  - supporting evidence?

- Will you use the knowledge gained to:
  - solve a problem?
  - write an essay?
  - compare the passage with other sources?
  - make notes or a summary?

When you have decided what you expect to gain, you can make certain you achieve your purpose.

What type of passage is it?

Activity

See if you can add three different types of writing to the list that we have begun below:

1 narratives – tell a story

2

3

4

You could have added: descriptions, explanations, arguments. Not all passages are just one of these types – they may be a mixture. However, by recognising the type of passage you are reading, you should be able to make sure that you tackle it in the right way and gain the maximum meaning from it. We will now look at how to tackle each type of passage.

Narrative

A narrative tells a story. To understand the story fully, you will need to identify and understand each event, and appreciate and remember the sequence of events. Bear in mind that writers sometimes introduce the conclusion of a story first and then narrate the sequence of events leading up to it.

Description

At the end of any descriptive passage, you will want to carry away a clear picture of the scene/person/event described. To understand and recall the writer's image, you will need to identify and concentrate on the key descriptive words and phrases.

Explanation

The points in an explanation are usually arranged in a logical order. You will need to identify and understand each step and follow the progression of steps if you are to gain real meaning from the passage.

Argument

You will need to appreciate each stage in an argument, and also be critical of the evidence presented. Is it accurate, relevant, sufficient? Is the argument balanced or is only one side being presented? By questioning the writer's argument in this way, you can gain a deeper understanding of it.

Activity

Read the passage below carefully. It is taken from Daphne du Maurier's *The Birds*. Decide what type of passage it is and then read it in the appropriate way so that you gain the maximum meaning from it. When you have finished, note down what you remember about it. Don't look back at the passage, but make your notes from memory.

> As he jumped the stile he heard the whirr of wings. A black-backed gull dived down at him from the sky, missed, swerved in flight and rose to dive again. In a moment it was joined by others, six, seven, a dozen, black-backed and herring mixed. Nat dropped his hoe. The hoe was useless. Covering his head with his arms he ran towards the cottage. They kept coming at him from the air, silent save for the beating wings. The terrible, fluttering wings. He could feel the blood on his hands, his wrists, his neck. Each stab of a swooping beak tore his flesh. If only he could keep them from his eyes. Nothing else mattered. He must keep them from his eyes. They had not learnt yet to cling to a shoulder, how to rip clothing, how to dive in mass upon the head, upon the body. But with each dive, with each attack, they became bolder. And they had no thought for themselves. When they dived low and missed, they crashed, bruised and broken, on the ground. As Nat ran he stumbled, kicking their spent bodies in front of him.

This is a descriptive passage but it is also a narrative, so we need to follow the stages of the story in order and concentrate on the descriptive words and phrases. You probably noted down something like:

> Nat attacked by one black-headed gull then a group. Hoe – useless. He ran towards the cottage trying to protect his head. The swooping beaks tore at his hands, wrists, neck. Nat stumbled over the spent bodies of those who had dived, missed and crashed, bruised and broken on the ground.

What is the structure of the passage?

'Structure' means 'arrangement of parts; how something is put together; its construction'.

When we look at any piece of writing and try to understand it, we should look for clues:

- the title – a good title will summarise what the passage is about;
- headings and subheadings – these will indicate which topic is going to be developed;
- individual words and what they mean;
- the make-up of each sentence and what it is saying;
- the construction of each paragraph;
- words providing links between the main part of each sentence and its supporting parts and between paragraphs.

The last two points are worth considering further.

Paragraphs

A paragraph is a group of sentences about one aspect of a subject. It should have a *key sentence* which introduces the paragraph. Usually this will be the first sentence, although it may occur at a later point. The rest of the sentences in the paragraph should support this key sentence. You may also find that the last sentence of the paragraph forms a link to the next paragraph.

In any longer piece of writing the paragraphs should form a logical progression. The first paragraph should introduce the subject; the following ones should develop it; the final paragraph should summarise what has been covered.

Activity

The passage below is taken from *Down There on a Visit*, by Christopher Isherwood. Read it carefully and then carry out the instructions that follow it:

> In the middle of the night I awoke, just as if somebody had roused me. Kneeling on my bunk, I peered out through the porthole. And there were the first lights of Germany shining across the black water, blue and green and red.
>
> Next morning we steamed up the river. Captain Dobson drank with the German pilot in the chartroom and became very cheerful. He had exchanged his old felt cap for a smart white cap, which made him look more than ever like a comic music-hall sea dog. We passed barges which were as snug as homes, with gay curtained windows and pots of flowers. Captain Dobson showed me various places of interest along the shore. Pointing to one factory building, he said, 'They've got hundreds of girls in there, cleaning the wool. It's so hot they strip to the waist.' He winked. I leered politely.
>
> In the harbour, the 'Coriolanus' became tiny again, as she made her way humbly to her berth amidst all the great ships. Captain Dobson shouted greetings at them as we passed, and was greeted in return. He appeared to be universally popular.
>
> When we tied up, our deck was so far below the level of the dock that the gangplank had to be nearly vertical. A police officer, who had come to inspect my passport, hesitated to descend it. Captain Dobson mocked him, 'Go 'vay, Tirpitz! Go 'vay!' He had called the pilot 'Tirpitz', too, and all the captains of the ships he had hailed. The police officer climbed down cautiously backwards, laughing but holding on very tight.
>
> After the stamping of the passport, there were no other formalities. I shook hands with the steward (who was sulking a little; a bad loser), tipped Teddy and waved good-bye to Captain Dobson. 'Give my love to the girls', he shouted from the bridge. The police officer obligingly came with me to the dock gates and put me on a tram which stopped outside Mr Lancaster's office.

Now:

- Underline the key sentence in each paragraph.
- Check that the rest of the sentences in each paragraph support each key sentence.
- Test your understanding of the passage by making notes in your notebook on everything you can remember about:
  (a) Captain Dobson;
  (b) the role of the police officer.

In this passage the first sentence of each paragraph is the key sentence, and the remaining sentences develop from this. Check back through the passage to ensure that you haven't missed out any key points about Captain Dobson and the police officer.

Linking words

Look carefully for words which link the main part of each sentence to its supporting parts and which link paragraphs together – words such as: 'although', 'because', 'since', 'unless', 'moreover', 'when'. These can provide vital clues to meaning. You can easily misread and misinterpret a passage if you make a mistake with link words.

Are you reading critically?

If you really understand a passage, you will be able to criticise it constructively, finding its good and bad points. It is important to question what you read, particularly when the writer is expressing his or her opinions.

Here are some useful questions to ask yourself:

- What is the writer's intention?
- Is the writer successful?
- How does the writer succeed?
- Who is the material intended for?
- Is it suitable for this audience?
- Is it arranged in a satisfactory/logical order?
- How could it be improved?
- Is it relevant?
- Is it sufficiently detailed/too detailed?

Review

- This unit has emphasised that careful reading involves active, critical reading – not just reading slowly and methodically.
- Aim to apply your comprehension skills to every aspect of a passage. Practise them by trying to gain more understanding from everything you read.
- When you have completed a piece of reading, ask yourself, 'What was it about?' Explain it to, or discuss it with, someone else. It's all too easy to just imagine that you have understood what you have read: the proof comes when you try to put this understanding into words.

UNIT 6
READING FOR RESEARCH

Targets

This unit will help you to:
- → improve your library skills;
- → use reference books more effectively;
- → extract information from books;
- → consider ways of recording your findings.

In this unit you will be looking at how you can develop your research skills. Research may not have played an important role in your past learning, but now schools, colleges and training organisations put more emphasis upon learners accessing information for themselves and organising their own studies.

Many of the activities in this unit invite you to consult information in a library. You may therefore find it helpful to study this unit in a college or public library. Alternatively, you can work through the unit as far as possible using the resources that are available to you, and then return to the activities that require access to a library as soon as you have the opportunity to spend some time in one.

Activity

Think about your own subject area. What research activities might you have to carry out? Note them down in your notebook before continuing.

You could have identified some or all of the following points:
- find books and magazines to use for background reading;
- extract information from various sources for essays and assignments;
- find meanings of unfamiliar or technical words in general or specialised dictionaries;
- find statistical evidence to support your opinions;
- locate relevant illustrations and maps;
- find names and addresses of other sources of information, such as government departments, pressure groups.

All of this information can be found in a library. Although staff will be willing to help you, your research will probably be more effective if you are able to use your own skills to gain the information you need.

Using your library

People are often surprised at the range of information and services that a library provides. A leaflet introducing my local library referred to books (of course!), newspapers, magazines, tapes, CDs, maps, leaflets on local and national issues, a business database, timetables, a local history collection, language courses on tape and video, photocopying and a fax machine.

Activity

> You might like to find out what your local and/or college library offers its users. If you do not have immediate access to a library there is no need to break off from your studies to do this now, but make a note in your notebook or diary of a time when you can go along and check. You may find it useful to make further notes in readiness for this visit as you work through the rest of this unit.

Knowing what your library offers will help you to make full use of it in your research, but you will also need to be able to locate books and information. You will need to know where fiction, non-fiction and reference books are kept, and be able to find any book that you need quickly and efficiently.

The following flow charts are designed to help you with this by giving you concrete examples.

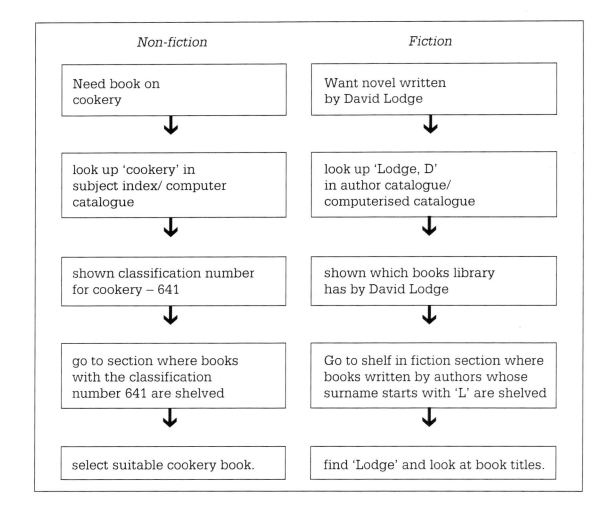

Every library should have a catalogue which will show all the books held by that library. In a computerised catalogue you can usually gain access to the information by keying in one of the following:

- the author's name;
- the title of the book;
- the subject;
- a key word in the title;
- the classification number.

If your library has a card catalogue or one on microfiches you will need to know either the author's surname or, if the book is non-fiction, the classification number of the book. You can find this number in the subject index, for example:

ENGLISH LANGUAGE DICTIONARIES   423

The classification number is the number shown on the spine of all non-fiction library books. This number represents the subject of the book. Each subject has a different number and all books with the same classification number (i.e., on the same subject) are arranged together on the shelf.

Activity

You might find it useful to use your local or college library's subject index to find the classification numbers of any subjects you are studying, your vocational/work area or any of your hobbies/interests. Then, using the classified catalogue, check which books the library has on these subjects.

Using reference books

So far in this unit we have been considering fiction and non-fiction books that can be borrowed. Reference books are shelved in a separate area of the library and may not be borrowed. Such books will probably be in constant use as people need them to check information rather than read them from cover to cover. You may find that reference books can help you in your research as they contain a wealth of general and specialised information.

Activity

Look at the books in the reference section of your library and, using your notebook:

1. List the types of books that are included in the reference section, such as:
    - general dictionaries;
    - yearbooks.
2. Note down any that you might find useful.
3. Note any difficulties that you can foresee in trying to get information from these books.

You will probably have found a wide variety of specialist dictionaries, encyclopaedias, directories, local and national government documents and bound collections of occupational and other journals. You will have seen that there are both general and subject-specific encyclopaedias, yearbooks and directories in the reference section.

You may have identified the following difficulties:

- It's sometimes hard to know where to look in a reference book for information.
- Reference books can be lengthy, detailed and sometimes full of obscure vocabulary.
- Sometimes it's difficult to see the purpose of the book and how it might help you.

Helping yourself

Here are some ways of tackling the problems we have just identified:

- Reference books are designed to be 'dipped into' to find a specific piece of information, so be clear in your own mind what you want to find out.
- You may find it helpful when researching to turn to general encyclopaedias first before you look at more specialised books. This will allow you to establish a firm foundation and will gradually introduce you to ideas.
- Use a general or specialised dictionary to help you with obscure vocabulary. Some reference books have a glossary of technical words.
- Try to familiarise yourself with the main reference books for your subject area. (See next section.) You will then be able to find information more efficiently, and to know the scope of each book and how it can help you in your research.

The layout of reference books

Many reference books, such as dictionaries and encyclopaedias, are arranged in alphabetical order. They may also have guide words at the top of each page. These show you the first and last word on that page and can help you as you scan through to find the relevant entry. To use a reference book which has a different way of organising the information, you will probably need to look at:

- the contents page (at the beginning of the book);
- the index (usually at the end);
- the preface or introduction, which should offer advice on how to use the book.

Skimming through the reference book will also allow you to become familiar with the organisation and scope of it.

Activity

Check which of the following reference books are held by your library. Select two or three and spend up to half an hour getting to know them. Focus particularly on how the contents are arranged. (We will also be asking you to consult these books in the next activity.)

- *Roget's Thesaurus*
- *Kelly's Business Directory*
- *Who's Who 1993*
- *The Oxford Dictionary of Quotations*
- *AA Hotels & Restaurants in Britain & Ireland*
- *The Oxford Dictionary of Art*
- *The Dictionary of Trade Name Origins*
- *Kempe's Engineers' Year Book.*

Finding and recording information

Whenever you need to find information from a reference book, think about whether you are:

- looking for information on a specific point;

or

- reading around the subject.

Your approach to the material should be different in each case. Let's look at this more fully.

Looking for information on a specific point

Before you consult the index or contents page, think about the *headings* under which the information that you need could be shown. Scan for those headings, but be prepared to look under different ones, too. (Unit 2 gives more help with scanning.)

Activity

Practise your skills at looking up information in reference books by finding the following information from the two or three books that you concentrated on for the last activity:

1. another word for 'pungent' (using *Roget's Thesaurus*)
2. the name and address of a local business that sells office furniture (*Kelly's Business Directory*)
3. when John Major became MP for Huntingdon (*Who's Who 1993*)
4. the name of the person who wrote 'Long is the day and hard' (*The Oxford Dictionary of Quotations*)
5. the name and address of a hotel in Fowey, Cornwall (*AA Hotels & Restaurants in Britain & Ireland*)
6. the title of a painting by William Bell Scott (*The Oxford Dictionary of Art*)
7. the origins of the Frisbee (*The Dictionary of Trade Name Origins*)
8. when the process of brazing was first discovered (*Kempe's Engineers' Year Book*).

Reading around a subject

You may need to gain information from a variety of sources and wish to skim through a selection of books first to see which ones will be most useful to you. If you start by looking at general books, you will find that many of these contain a bibliography – a booklist which will direct you to more specialised materials. Having skimmed through a book, you will then need to read the relevant sections more carefully and probably make notes. Your notes will help you to combine ideas from a number of sources and you can refer to them at a later date. (Unit 5 gives more advice about careful reading.)

Making notes

Whichever method of recording information you use, you must ensure that your notes are meaningful without being too wordy. You shouldn't copy whole sentences from your sources unless you are using these quotations to support your own ideas. In this case you must show who you are quoting and where you obtained the quotation from. There are two main types of notes, *linear* and *diagrammatic*.

Linear notes

These are the conventional way of making notes, with headings and subheadings to introduce and separate points. Many learners find it helpful to indent information and to number points to make the notes easier to follow. Here's an example:

> Financial Transactions
> 1 Petty Cash
> For:
>   – small amounts
>   – day-to-day expenditure
> Recording systems
>   (a) Imprest system shows:
>   – debits & credits
>   – dates
>   – details
>   – balance

Diagrammatic notes

These are more visual. Some learners find them particularly useful as a basis for revision. Here's an example:

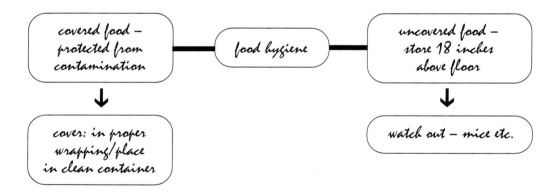

Review

Good research skills are a valuable asset. If you are new to research then set yourself goals, for example:

- Become aware of sources of information for your subject.
- Become a confident and competent library user.
- Make sure you can find your way around useful books within your subject area
- Find a method of recording your research notes that you find helpful.

UNIT 7

STUDY AREAS

Targets

This unit will help you to:

→ identify the reading requirements of different subject areas;

→ analyse the reading requirements of your own subject/s.

When you are studying, you will find information and ideas presented to you in many different formats, for example, continuous writing, tables, graphs, diagrams, plans. Your purposes in reading will also vary. Sometimes you might need to gather facts; at other times you will want to understand the writer's intention, to select relevant points or to evaluate or be able to interpret information. Reading requirements vary according to the subject and the type of material that you are working on.

In this unit you will be looking at several subject areas and their reading requirements. We have not been able to cover every study area, but the unit should help you to think about the reading requirements of your own subject/s.

English literature

Most of the reading you will do in this subject will be concerned with novels, short stories, poems and plays. However, you may also be asked to study such things as film or television scripts, biographies, travel writing, personal diaries. In your background reading, you may also read critical appraisals of the texts you are studying.

Examiners often complain that learners read literature at a very superficial level, for example, gaining an impression of a story but no insight into how the writer uses language or develops characters and plot.

In novels you may be asked to think about the way the writer presents the plot, the pace of the story and where climaxes occur. You will be looking at the structure of the story, not just at events. You should also evaluate and consider other aspects of the work, for example, the writer's intention: what message or moral is he or she trying to convey?

In poetry you will be particularly concerned with the writer's use of language. You will also need to understand terms like 'figurative language' and 'imagery', and be able to appreciate what the writer hopes to convey through his/her language. All of this can be achieved if you study the text carefully and read it critically.

Activity

Study this extract from a poem by Philip Larkin:

Money

Quarterly, is it, money reproaches me:
'Why do you let me lie here wastefully?
I am all you never had of goods and sex.
You could get them still by writing a few cheques.'

So I look at others, what they do with theirs:
They certainly don't keep it upstairs.
By now they've a second house and car and wife:
Clearly money has something to do with life
— In fact, they've a lot in common, if you enquire:
You can't put off being young until you retire,
And however you bank your screw, the money you save
Won't in the end buy you more than a shave.

Does Larkin seem to regret his cautious attitude to money and life here? Why?

Do you gain the impression that he is an 'on-looker' marvelling at other people's ability to use money to acquire material goods, and even, wives? Why?

If you have the opportunity, compare notes on your responses to this activity with other learners or with your tutor.

Sociology

Information in this subject is often presented in the form of statistics. You will need to study the figures carefully but you probably won't want to comment upon all the information. Usually you will be interpreting trends and indicating significant features.

Activity

The statistics below show unemployment rates within certain countries. The data was collected from surveys carried out during 1985 and 1986. What could you conclude from this information?

	Unemployment rates					
	Austria	West Germany	Britain	Italy	USA	Switzerland
Men	3.9%	4.5%	12.7%	4.7%	3.9%	0.4%
Women	6.5%	6.3%	11.9%	6.9%	3.7%	2.0%
Aged under 25	6.7%	7.1%	21.7%	17.8%	5.9%	4.3%
Aged 24–44	4.4%	6.0%	9.9%	4.6%	3.2%	0.3%
Aged 45+	4.3%	3.3%	10.7%	1.4%	4.5%	0.4%
All	4.9%	5.1%	12.4%	5.4%	3.8%	0.9%

Notes. The percentage bases are all those who defined themselves as 'in paid work' or 'unemployed'. Swiss data are from 1987.

From *British Social Attitudes*, Special International Report

You should have noted that:

- Unemployment rates were highest in Britain and lowest in Switzerland.
- Female unemployment was generally higher than male unemployment.
- In all countries the under-25s were most affected by unemployment.

You could give examples from the table to support and expand these points, but these are the trends that need to be highlighted.

Geography

While you will have to understand written and tabular information, an important part of any geography course will be the interpretation of maps, plans and even photographs.

Activity

> Spend a moment thinking about maps. What reading skills might they involve?

Our suggestions are that you need to understand: signs/symbols to denote buildings etc.; contour lines or shading to represent land formations; scale; grids and map references. You will also need to be able to visualise the map as a three-dimensional landscape.

You will also, of course, need to feel confident about your map-reading skills and practise using them.

Business Studies

In this subject learners are often asked to carry out research on local or national business issues. While your tutor will give you suggestions about how to approach this, you will need to use reference books to find company names and details, for example, *Yellow Pages*; *Kelly's Business Directory*; *Who Owns Whom*; *Directory of Trademarks*.

The information you collect will have to be organised and the relevant points selected. You may have to analyse information and make judgements, so a critical reading style is essential.

Technology

Information in this subject is often presented in diagrams. It can be tempting to skim through these and concentrate on the main text, but diagrams should be examined closely. The following activity will help you to appreciate how you can deal with diagrams.

Activity

> Study the diagram on mild steel at the top of the next page. If any of the vocabulary is unfamiliar to you, check its meaning in your dictionary. Think carefully about the information shown:
>
> - Which boxes show the uses of mild steel?
>
> - What other sorts of information are given?

(continued overleaf)

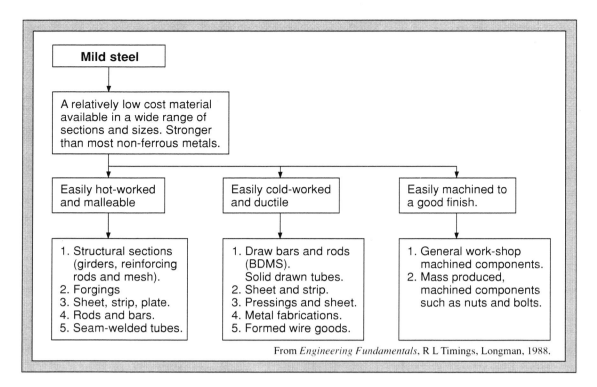

From *Engineering Fundamentals*, R L Timings, Longman, 1988.

You will have seen that the boxes at the bottom of the diagram show the uses of mild steel. The other information provided includes brief details about the cost and advantages of mild steel.

To gain a clear understanding of a diagram:

- Concentrate on the vocabulary.
- Extract the main points.
- Rephrase these in your own words.

Activity

We suggest you think further about the reading requirements of the subject/s or vocational area you are studying. When you have considered these, note down what reading approaches you could adopt to cope with these effectively.

Review

Although we have not covered all aspects of reading for study purposes in this unit, you should now have a clearer view of:

- the reading approaches required for materials which give information in various formats;
- the reading demands of your own study area/s.

UNIT 8

REVIEWING PROGRESS

Targets

This unit will help you to:
→ consider the reading approaches you need to use in exams;
→ review what you have achieved by working through these units;
→ identify the opportunities for reading that are open to you;
→ decide where you will go from here.

Reading and examinations

In Unit 1 we referred to comments made by examiners about candidates' reading. For example:

- Candidates frequently fail to read questions exactly.
- Some candidates fail to recognise what is asked.
- Candidates fail to pay attention to 'explain'.
- Many candidates lack the ability to summarise and to select adequately.
- Candidates ought to recognise not only the shape of the question but also the appropriate register being called for.

Such comments are made by examiners every year when they bemoan the fact that candidates throw away marks by not reading the exam paper carefully. When you are in an exam there is always a danger of feeling so nervous and pressurised that you forget to follow certain golden rules:

- Read the whole exam paper thoroughly.
- Check carefully the number of questions to be attempted and the time allowed. (Make a note of these if it helps you to focus on them.)
- Decide which questions you will attempt.
- Re-read these questions, underlining all the key words and phrases.
- Pay particular attention to how you have been asked to respond, i.e., look for words like 'describe', 'analyse'. (We'll be thinking more about these words later in this unit.)
- Note whether the question has more than one part to it.
- Read each question again before you plan your answer.
- Read the question after you have finished planning. Check that you have covered all the points and that your answer is relevant.
- In English exams, you will need to consider whether the question indicates what tone your writing should adopt. For example, if you have you been asked to write a formal letter you should use a formal tone.

45

Activity

Note down next to each of the following words what you think examiners mean when they ask you to:

describe:

comment upon:

compare:

discuss:

evaluate:

explain:

illustrate:

analyse:

differentiate:

summarise:

Our suggestions are:
- describe: to give details about an event, situation or process;
- comment upon: give your opinion about;
- compare: find similarities between two or more things;
- discuss: give points for and against;
- evaluate: assess or judge the issues;
- explain: usually requires you to give reasons for an action or happening;
- illustrate: provide examples of in order to clarify or explain;
- analyse: consider the various aspects;
- differentiate: show the differences between;
- summarise: sum up without including too many details.

UNIT 8 REVIEWING PROGRESS

What have you achieved?

We hope you have enjoyed working through these units and that you feel your reading has improved.

Activity

At this stage, it is a good idea to review your achievements. Think about the areas you have covered and now feel more confident about. You may like to note these down below.

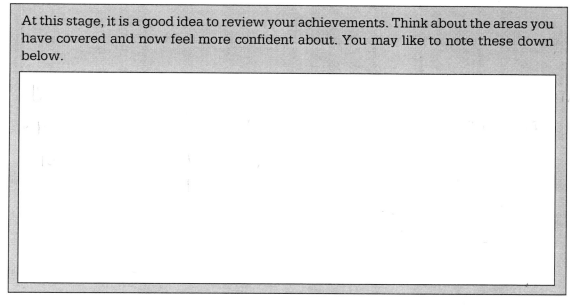

Here are some possibilities. You may feel that you:

- are able to use a wider variety of reading approaches (Units 2 and 4);
- have learnt ways of coping with difficult texts (Unit 3);
- are more aware of a writer's intentions (Units 4 and 5);
- are more able to distinguish fact from opinion (Unit 4);
- are more confident about using a library (Unit 6);
- can deal with the reading requirements of your study area more effectively (Unit 7).

If there are any points from the above list about which you feel less than confident, you should review the relevant units again.

Making more opportunities

Activity

Look back to the review section at the end of Unit 1 where we advised you to read widely and to approach reading in an organised way. Think about your reading habits now. How have you acted on this suggestion? If there are any points to which your answer is 'no', make a resolution now to put this advice into practice in future.

Where next?

However much progress you have made, you can continue to extend your reading. Here are some suggestions:

- We have not given you specific advice on reading for pleasure, but this form of reading has many benefits. For example, your writing skills will improve as you become more aware of the way others express themselves.

- Try to read books in subject areas that are new to you.

- You can find out about writers and subjects that are new to you by:

  - listening to book review programmes, short stories, plays and poetry on the radio;

  - reading the review sections of magazines and newspapers;

  - browsing around libraries, bookshops and your friends' bookshelves.

We are sure you will find that once you acquire the reading habit it opens up new horizons that you would never previously have dreamt of.

Good luck and good reading!

READING

ASSIGNMENTS FOR TUTORIAL COMMENT

Reading

Introduction

These assignments are intended for learners studying with an NEC tutor. Each of the assignments should be carried out at the point indicated. You should send an assignment to your tutor as soon as you have completed all its parts. Your tutor will mark your answers and give you personal help. He or she will also deal with any difficulties you meet, and help you to adapt the course to suit your own circumstances.

Treat each assignment as a further step to learning. Don't worry about making mistakes; the word 'error' originally meant 'wandering about looking for something'. It is through making errors that we learn things and find what it is that we are looking for. However, if you feel unsure of how to respond to a question, write to your tutor and ask for advice. While you are waiting for a reply, go on to the next Unit.

Bear in mind the contribution that your family and friends can make to your learning. Discuss ideas with them and if possible persuade them to read your assignments and comment on them before you send them to your tutor.

How to present your assignments

Please follow these instructions for all your assignments.

1 Leave a margin of one and a half inches (about 4cm) on the left side of the page and three inches (about 8cm) along the bottom. This space is for your tutor's comments.

2 If you are not typing your assignments, make sure that your handwriting is clear. Use pen not pencil.

3 Number each question clearly.

Note: As an NEC learner you will need to work through the course-book from start to finish. You should therefore ignore any suggestions to work though the material in a different order, or to omit Units.

ASSIGNMENT A

Send this assignment to your tutor when you have completed Unit 1

1 On page 8 of Unit 1 we ask you to keep a record of what you have read in a recent 24-hour period, and to consider how you read each item. Send to your tutor a note of your response to this activity. Accompany it with a list of what you consider to be your three most frequent reasons for reading. The list in the activity on page 10 may help you with this.

2 We would also like you to send to your tutor the action plan which we invite you to complete at the bottom of page 10. As an NEC student you will need to work through the course book from start to finish, but your plan will still provide your tutor with a clearer idea of your own priority areas.

Reading

ASSIGNMENT B

Complete the first part of this assignment when you reach the end of Unit 2, and the second part when you reach the end of Unit 3.

Part 1

Unit 2 discusses the two reading methods known as skimming and scanning. We would like you to demonstrate your grasp of skimming as follows:

1. Choose a passage which is factual and which covers up to two sides of A4 (the equivalent of half a side of a tabloid newspaper).
2. Then skim the passage. Write out some brief notes of what you have found out from your skim.

If you found any problems in practising either skimming *or* scanning, explain to your tutor in a short note what these were.

Part 2

For Part 2 we would again like you to select a short (50–100 words) passage that you can cut out or photocopy and send to your tutor. This passage should be one that you have found it difficult to understand. With the passage send to your tutor answers to the following questions:

1. Of the techniques listed at the bottom of page 19, which did you find most helpful?
2. Write out the passage in your own words, in a way which makes it easier for you to understand. Send your rewrite to your tutor along with the original.
3. Select between three and six words that caused you difficulty when you first encountered the passage. Write out brief explanations of their meaning in a way that makes sense to you.

Assignment C

Carry out Part 1 of this assignment when you have completed Unit 4 and Part 2 when you have completed Unit 5.

Part 1

In Unit 4 we consider four types of language that are frequently used in everyday writing. For this part of the assignment we would like you to search out examples of these and send them to your tutor. Your best source is likely to be a tabloid newspaper. If you do not usually read one you should make a point of buying two or three different papers on the same day. Search through them for two examples each of:

- purely factual language
- opinion
- persuasive language
- emotive language.

If possible these should come from a single report or piece of writing, which you can cut out and send to your tutor. You can indicate the different sorts of language by underlining in differently coloured pens or pencils: black for fact, blue for opinion, green for persuasive language and red for emotive language. Accompany your sample text with a note of:

- what your feel is the writer's overall intention
- whether you feel the opinion expressed is justified
- what the persuasive language is trying to persuade you to think or do
- what feeling the emotive language is intended to arouse.

Your notes should be no more than one side of A4 (less if your writing is small). Do make it clear to your tutor which features of the passage you are referring to.

Part 2

1. For part 2 we would first like you to send to your tutor your notes in response to the activity on page 33. Carry out the instructions that precede and follow the passage, and make your notes before reading on to the final paragraph on page 33. You may wish to amend your work once you have read our own comments in the text, but you should still send your tutor your initial notes, as well as any later changes.

2. We would now like you to carry out a critical reading exercise on a passage of your choice. This should ideally be a newspaper or magazine article which you can either cut out or photocopy and send to your tutor. Try to find a subject that interests you, and which is covered in no more than one page – half a page if you are using a broadsheet newspaper. Use the checklist on page 34 as guide, and send to your tutor your notes in answer to each point (you may wish to omit any points that you feel are not applicable). Your own notes should cover about one side of A4 in total – more if your writing is larger than average.

Reading

ASSIGNMENT D

Carry out this assignment when you have completed Unit 6.

For this assignment we would like you to visit your local library as suggested in
Unit 6. On page 37 we suggest two activities that aim to help you identify ways in which the library can help you in your work or studies. Send to your tutor notes in response to:

- both parts of the first activity – ie provide a short list of classification numbers and a list of up to six books that you might find useful
- all three parts of the second activity – although you should aim to spend most time on (2) and (3).

Assignment E

Carry out Part 1 of this assignment when you have completed Unit 7 and Part 2 when you have completed Unit 8.

Part 1

On page 44 we ask you to think further about the reading requirements of the subject(s) or vocational areas that you are studying. When you have done this we suggest you note down what reading approaches you could adopt to cope with these requirements effectively. When you have completed your notes send them to your tutor for comment, adding a note of any special challenges posed by your reading tasks.

Part 2

On pages 47 to 48 we suggest some ways of reviewing your progress on this course and invite you to make further plans. You will find it helpful to receive your tutor's comment on your response to these questions, which we repeat in a single list below:

- What areas covered in the course do you now feel more confident about?

- What areas covered in the course do you feel less than confident about? (Be as specific as possible here.)

- Have you followed the suggestion in Unit 1 to read widely and in an organised way? If there are any points which you feel you could work at further, make a note of these.

- In what ways are you planning to find out more about writers and subjects that are new to you? (Again be as specific as possible.)

Your notes in answer to these questions should cover no more than one side of A4 – less if your handwriting is small.

Index

Argument		31
Comprehension		29–30
Critical reading		34
Description		31, 32
Difficult texts		19–22
	background reading	20
	careful reading	19–20
	meaning of words	21–22
	put into own words	21
	split into parts	20–21
Effective reading		10–11
Emotive		24, 28
Explanation		31
Fact		24–25
How you read		8
Information	finding	39
	recording	40
Library		36
Narrative		31
Opinion		24, 26
Paragraphs		32–34
Persuade		24, 26–27
Reference books	layout	38
	using	37
Research		36
Scanning		12, 15–17
Skimming		12–15
Structure		32
Tables		42
What you read		7
Why you read		9
	for study	41

© National Extension College